Mrs. Katie Smith-Myott
767 Scheffer Ave.
Saint Paul, MN 55102

D1550775

JOAN CHITTISTER

WE ARE ALL

Reflections on Unity, Community
and Commitment to Each Other

**TWENTY-THIRD
PUBLICATIONS**
twentythirdpublications.com

TWENTY-THIRD PUBLICATIONS
One Montauk Avenue, Suite 200
New London, CT 06320
(860) 437-3012 or (800) 321-0411
www.twentythirdpublications.com

ISBN: 978-1-62785-366-8
Library of Congress Control Number: 2018936575
Printed in the U.S.A.

A division of Bayard, Inc.

Contents

JOAN CHITTISTER *is an internationally known author, lecturer, and visionary voice in church and society. She has written more than 50 books and received numerous awards for her writings and work on behalf of peace, justice, and women's rights. She is executive director of Benetvision, a resource center for contemporary spirituality, and the guiding force of Monasteries of the Heart, an online movement sharing Benedictine spirituality with contemporary seekers. Sister Joan is an online columnist for the* **National Catholic Reporter** *and co-chairs the Global Peace Initiative of Women. She is past president of the Leadership Conference of Women Religious (LCWR) and a former prioress of the Benedictine Sisters of Erie.*

INTRODUCTION

Life, we learn young, is one long, unending game of push and pull. One part of us pushes us always toward wholeness, toward a sense of connection with the universe which, in the very act of engagement with the human community, brings us a sense of peace. We are not here as isolates, we realize. We are here to become community. We are on an odyssey with potentiality, and we know it. We have been foreordained to make humanity more humane.

The other part of us, however, pulls us back into ourselves. It separates us from the universe around us and leaves us feeling distant and out of sync. We lack

1

the sense of kinship that the human family is a family. It deprives us of the universal concern that drives us beyond ourselves to the center of humankind. It leaves us without what it means to be a person with a purpose, a human being whose search is for the ultimate human experience for us all.

Worse, this struggle for unity is an eternal one.

And yet, it is this very paradox of life that stretches us not only to grow but to contribute to the growth of the rest of the universe around us.

We say we seek unity, yes. But lurking within every human act is the gnawing need to be independent, to think of ourselves as distinct from the rest of life. We allow ourselves to be deluded into thinking of ourselves as superior to everything around us, in control of everything and everyone we touch.

Indeed, this search for the fullness of the self is the razor's edge, the teeter-totter, the high-wire act that is the final measure of our happiness, our consciousness of what it actually means to be human. More, it is the answer to the great questions of life: Why am I here? What am I supposed to be doing? What is the spiritual purpose of existence?

It is a spiritual battle for the center of the soul.

Is the purpose of the gift of life to consume it for ourselves, to remake it in our own name? Or is our purpose to join the human race on its way to fullness of life for everyone? Is it to give my life back to Creation safe and undefined? Or is my role in life to be part of knitting life together for everyone so that we are all forever safe?

The struggle between the two sets of choices is an eternal one. The greatest question of them all haunts us: Whatever the battle, is the battle winnable?

This simple little book touches on four elements of mindfulness that account for all the angst in our society right now—moral maturity, spiritual witness, personal greatness, and universal kinship. These are the things that determine whether or not we go through life as part of its solution or part of the weight on its progress.

The choice is actually simple. We must only decide if we will go on lingering in the shadows of life, forever trying to choose between doing what a numbed world will call "nice," or step up and, in the face of evil, proclaim instead what is right.

CHAPTER ONE

*I firmly believe that our salvation
depends on the poor.*

DOROTHY DAY

Who Will Save Us?

This insight itself is a kind of life-changer. The heart stops for a moment as the words sink in. It is, at the very least, certainly a soul-stretcher. We begin to look again at the way we see the world.

Even more than that, perhaps, it changes our very sense of the purpose and direction of our lives.

It takes a while, in fact, to process the words: Our salvation depends on the poor? Surely that's impossible. A kind of holy exaggeration. Our salvation depends on ourselves.

No, actually not. Not if we rethink some of the things we know about life.

Like everything else in life, the very concept of work has evolved over the centuries. We've gone from communal farming in agricultural communities to individual positions based on individual interests or opportunities in a money economy. As a result, of course, our social systems over time began to look very different. Except for one thing. The fact is that whatever work we do, we still work for the reasons people have always worked. We work to maintain ourselves. We earn our bread by the sweat of our hands, *The Rule of Benedict* tells us in the sixth century.

But more than that, we also work to maintain the planet itself: "Till the land and keep it," scripture commands us in Genesis. We're not put here, we come to understand, to exploit the land or threaten the life of the planet. We are to develop it and protect it. We are to take responsibility for the creation we've been given.

At the same time, we work driven by the internal need to develop ourselves—our interests and our talents. We are to create with the creator, to bring ourselves to the fullness of ourselves just as we are to develop the rest of creation.

And yet, despite the obvious, despite the fact that humans are obviously interdependent, we struggle between becoming fully human and being spiritually underdeveloped. The issue that is most in question, actually in danger, in a highly individualistic society, is whether we must also work to care for the rest of humanity, as well. And, if not, what will happen to those who cannot find work that enables them to care for themselves? And what will happen to the quality of our own humanity, as well?

What kind of human, human beings, shall we become if we become human for ourselves alone?

We must work, in other words, to develop the human community itself.

Work, you see, is bigger than ourselves. Work is a community responsibility, a community act, a community gift. But therein lies the problem. In a highly competitive, capitalist society, the new capitalist scripture is that "God helps those who help themselves." Which is pious code for "In the end, it's all up to you—and you are on your own."

Unfortunately, that will be each of us before life is over. And then what? Then, like everyone else who is alone and unprotected on our streets right now and waiting for help from us, we will be alone and unprotected. Then, we will be the ones needing help. And where will that help come from if not from those who know their own salvation depends on their willingness to help others?

Scripture is clear: We are taught to "do unto others as we would have others do unto us." (Matthew 7:12)

"Being our brother's and sister's keeper" is about more than praying for the salvation of a set of disembodied souls. We are not bifurcated human beings, part body, part soul. Whatever we do, we do wholly. Or, as N.T. Wright says, "The work of salvation, in its full sense, is about whole human beings, not merely souls."

There are as many ways of being saved as there are of being lost. Then we all need someone special, someone committed to helping us save ourselves. Mother Teresa says, "If we have no peace, it is because we have forgotten that we belong to each other."

Sometimes we feel sad, out of touch with the world around us, depressed. The people who refuse to allow us to surrender to the undertows of life are our saviors.

———————————

Only those who can help us remember that life itself is a gift too precious to waste can bring us back to the fullness of ourselves. Our saviors are not people with magical life skills. They are people who help us to make the best out of life as it is.

———————————

To see those in need and do nothing is to become a little less human ourselves.

———————————

Do not hesitate to weep and cry for those who weep and cry in front of us. The tears we shed for the pains of others are a measure of our own humanity.

———————————

The memory of being helped by someone else in our own lives is what prepares us to help another. "What you remember," W.S. Merwin writes, "saves you."

———————————

What others have generously done for us is what obligates us to do the same. As Jane Addams taught, "The good we secure for ourselves is precarious and uncertain until it is secured for all and incorporated into our common life."

The whole human community is waiting for each of us to redeem our unpaid debts of help and care and unearned love. Then, the poor of the world may also, like us, know the gratuitous love of God.

The poor give themselves to us asking for nothing in return but an awareness of their humanity and everything to which it entitles them.

To fail to respond to the poor around us makes the entire world a more sterile, inhuman place. What's even more true, it marks us as a little less developed ourselves. Martin Buber teaches, "A person cannot approach the divine by reaching beyond the human. To become human is what this individual person has been created for."

To save the poor it is necessary to love the poor. Not because they are poor but because no one is meant to be poor in a world of plenty.

If some people are destitute, it is because others have been dulled by affluence. Then we become just one more "Let them eat cake" society where the secure simply assume that the poor are poor because they want to be. As if the poor do not have the needs, the desires, the hopes of us all.

What we do not take responsibility for will become the new normal that destroys us all. Aleksandr Solzhenitsyn writes, "The salvation of humankind lies only in making everything the concern of all."

The distorted ideas we have about what it means to be a society, what it means to be a human being, what it means to be alive determines what the world itself will become. "Fight to escape from your own cleverness," John Climacus writes. "If you do, then you will find salvation."

We grow up a little at a time. And in the same manner, we grow interiorly—spiritually—a little at a time. But to ignore our spiritual development is to diminish our own becoming as well as affect the lives of those who need us. "You cannot dream yourself into a character," James Froude says. "You must hammer and forge yourself one."

The poor call us to love as God loves—with reckless generosity and despite merit. They take our self-centeredness and challenge it to the fullness of its humanity.

Only what we do for the poor will count toward the valuation of our own humanity.

To ignore the poor is to ignore the very quality of human life in general. "Love and compassion are necessities," the Dalai Lama writes, "not luxuries. Without them, humanity cannot survive."

What we do and do not do for the poor will determine the level of our own existence. When we provide for others, we enrich ourselves. We become better, bigger souls; deeper, truer hearts.

The old clothes we give away will not change the nature of life for many. It will only warm them one more day as they go on dying. It's what we do to end the dying that counts. "Every day," Che Guevara writes, "you have to fight so that love for humanity can be transformed into concrete deeds."

It's what we set out to do to raise the quality of life for everyone that will, in the end, define what it means to be really human. "We cannot trample upon the humanity of others," Chinua Achebe writes, "without devaluing our own."

Evolution, they say, is not over. It is an ongoing state of life. The only question is, Have we ourselves reached its peak, or is there still hope for humanity as a species?

Jewish wisdom teaches that, "To save one life, it is as if you have saved the world." None of us can save the world, but by saving just one other person we can show the rest of the world how it's done. Dag Hammarskjöld writes, "It is more noble to give yourself completely to one individual than to labor diligently for the salvation of the masses."

Only those who live for others as well as for themselves ever really live at all.

To be caught in the trap of the self is to struggle forever and not become much of a human being at all. "There are too many people," Robert Zend writes, "and too few human beings."

The poor are not the "other." They are myself in different circumstances. They remind me that I am only one incident away from losing what I think I am entitled to. Walt Whitman writes, "I do not ask the wounded person how they feel; I myself become the wounded person."

It is one thing to talk about caring for the poor, it's another to work to make it happen—even in our own town, our own institutions, our own country. "If you want to make a difference," Brené Brown says, "the next time you see someone being cruel to another human being, take it personally."

The needs of the other are the situations in life that expose the degree of sanctity and salvation we have managed by this moment in life to develop.

"Beauty will save the world," Dostoyevsky writes. But not unless that beauty is seeded within us, flowers in the way we walk through the world, and becomes a beacon of the possible to those around us.

FOR A LISTENING HEART

I firmly believe that our salvation depends on the poor. DOROTHY DAY

Spend a few minutes with this quote and then ask yourself:

- What do these words say to me? What feelings or memories do the words evoke in me?

- What do these words say about my spiritual journey?

- My journal response to this quote is:

*Dorothy Day, Obl. OSB (1897-1980) was one of four great Americans singled out by Pope Francis when he addressed a joint session of the US Congress, September 2015. With Peter Maurin, she founded the Catholic Worker in New York City, a pacifist movement that continues to combine direct aid for the poor and homeless with gospel-based nonviolent direct action on their behalf. She served as editor of the **Catholic Worker** newspaper from 1933 until her death. She was a Catholic convert, a Benedictine oblate, an organizer for the rights of the poor, a pacifist, a suffragist, a journalist, and a proponent of civil disobedience. For information on the effort for her canonization, see dorothydayasaint.org.*

CHAPTER TWO

*Dedication to God means dedication
to the **whole** of creation.*

EDITH STEIN

Holy Co-creation

Funny, isn't it. Most of us were raised to believe exactly the opposite of Saint Edith Stein's insight about what it takes to be "dedicated to God." We were raised to think that "dedication to God" meant withdrawal from anything but God. As if such a thing as withdrawal from everything in the real world could possibly be achieved. Whatever it was genuine withdrawal was supposed to mean.

But we all knew without a doubt that dedication to God had to have something to do with separation from the rest of the world. It surely meant withdrawal from other people. It certainly meant withdrawal from the cares of the world. It definitely meant withdrawal from the dirty side of life.

In fact, it meant withdrawal from whatever might be a distraction from the "Holy Ghost" that is the God who hovers over us but whom we cannot grasp, cannot see, and, in the end, hope to win for ourselves regardless of what happens to everybody else around us.

Salvation—our own personal, private, and decidedly individualistic project—was a most intimate and exclusive operation. Life was an exercise called the relationship between God and me. My part was to be silent, otherworldly, and centered on eternity. God's part was to grade me accordingly.

Edith Stein, philosopher, convert from Judaism, mystic of the meaning of life, knew better. With one sweep of the pen, she blows away religion based primarily on the sanctification of the self. Ironically, it is the spirituality of creation—our affinity, our care, for the rest of creation—that really stretches us to the wholeness of ourselves and to the wholeness of God, as well. In fact, come to think about it, what else can?

Only when we see ourselves, humans, as part of creation, rather than as the crown of creation, will we ever be able to come anywhere close to really grasping the greatness of God and God's gifts to us. Only then will we begin to see the glowing face of God everywhere. Only then will we begin to understand that we are all meant to come to fullness of life together—plants, animals, planet, and humans in one great reciprocal circle of a common creation. Until we do, she contends, all of us will go on living life with spiritual blinders.

What we do not do to save the whole of creation will shrink our own spiritual vision and separate us, starved and emaciated in soul, from the wholeness of life. We will look at forests and, like the loggers destroying the rain forests on this earth, fail to see the living gift of them. We will take for granted the devotion of our pets and fail to recognize that real human relationships are about more than sex or social comfort or authority. We will watch our children grow up in cement jungles, denied the right to plant tomatoes or the wonder of picking flowers. We will find innocent enemies and set out to destroy them rather than protect them as sisters and brothers and make them our friends. No wonder we are a culture that pollutes our waters, poisons our land, threatens to vaporize our enemies, and so annihilates our future rather than protects it.

Saint Edith Stein, a Jewish nun living under Nazi oppression, proclaimed then what few cared about and even fewer knew: what we do to the rest of creation we do to ourselves. What we destroy in the rest of creation makes it even easier to destroy our own.

But God sees the despoliation of all that is "good" and comes closer to those who are its saviors. And therein lies the secret of both the quality of our "dedication" and the depth of our relationship with God. Why? Because it's profitable to steward the world well? No. Because it is holy to care for the world as God cares for the world. Because co-creation is the task of being human.

Evolution is the science of the oneness of creation. To deny any part of it is to deny the creation of humankind, as well.

Nature is the call to the depth of the self, to our very communion with all of life.

Evolution is a way of creation, not the denial of the Creator God. The evolutionary God links us to the rest of creation rather than separates us from it.

Evolution does not mean that human beings are animals only, but it does make humans conscious of our indebtedness to the rest of the animal world. For if humans are valuable, then so are animals from whose gifts evolved our own as we grew beyond them. "Until we stop harming all other living beings, we are still savages," Thomas A. Edison writes.

For almost a billion years after the earth was bathed in the elements of life, scientists tell us that nothing perceptible was happening. The chemistry of the earth was preparing itself. But then the life forms that populated the world as we know it appeared. If we are meant to learn anything from that, in an instant-gratification world, it must surely be patience with the process of life.

It's what we know about evolution that gives us grounds for humility. First, human beings come late to this world and, second, they come totally dependent on its organisms and animals for survival. Or, as Kurt Vonnegut says of the situation, "I was taught that the human brain was the crowning glory of evolution so far, but I think it's a very poor scheme for survival."

It is not our kind of life that counts where the world is concerned, it is the whole web of life that is important to us all.

It is the way we live with the rest of life that determines the quality of our own. After all, other life forms don't need us. We need them. And besides all that, as George Eliot says, "Animals are such agreeable friends—they ask no questions, they pass no criticism."

We need to understand that what we do to nature, we do to ourselves. But there is not a chance that we will stop clogging the air with pollution, the seas with garbage, and the land with chemicals until it hurts us. Not a chance, that is, until the pollution makes breathing impossible, the fish sick, and the vegetables full of poison.

We are so enamored with our "superiority" that we fail

to see our inclination to species-specific suicide. Our arrogance as a species increases while the glaciers melt and the ground turns to dust. What kind of human spiritual development is that?

———

The animals that sustain us know us to be their chief predator. They provide our food, our fur, our rugs, our work animals, and our research subjects. William Ralph Inge writes, "We...have treated our distant cousins in fur and feather so badly that, beyond doubt, if they were able to formulate a religion, they would depict the Devil in human form."

———

We have taken ourselves out of nature to the point that whatever happens to nature has little or no meaning to us. We don't know in the center of our souls that ice melting in Antarctica may well destroy our beaches, our homes, our important wetlands. We have lost a part of our own soul as a result.

———

Animals are models of us, raw and open about it. They stand before us without all the constraints that come with rationality which we ourselves often abandon.

They bring us all the sensitivity they have without the barriers of propriety. They show us to ourselves.

Nature has so much to teach us. In an urban world, however, finding enough of it to really learn from is difficult. We are humans alienated from the very earth of which we are part.

Life is one thing; consciousness is another. And human consciousness was thirteen billion years in coming. But what a glorious moment that was.

As Tom Robbins writes, "We are in this life to enlarge the soul, to liberate the spirit, and to light up the brain." The very thought of taking all that time in our development and then going through life with small souls, enslaved spirits, and dulled-down brains is misfortune without meaning.

It's not death that is the tragedy of life. It's going through life without ever having fully awakened in mind and soul that is the tragedy.

Nature never meant for people to be hungry, dispossessed, and drinking polluted water. Nature yields more than enough for every person on earth to live a decent life. So what's stopping that?

Q Q Q

The whole thought of wrenching nature for our puny little selves is one of the remaining great ethical questions of our time. Jeremy Bentham puts it this way: "The question is not, Can they [animals] reason? nor, Can they talk? but, Can they suffer?" And the answer is…? So why do we keep on doing it?

Q Q Q

To have a favorite stream and watch it turn brown and thick with garbage is to watch life as we have known it begin to die. Worse, it is to watch it wither and dry up at our own hands.

Q Q Q

Nature is the first step toward the mystical. No wonder so many nations fail at humanity when they can no longer care for the plant and animal parts of their own lives.

Q Q Q

What we teach children about the way to care for the earth, to protect the animals, to maintain the land will protect them a great deal more than what they learn from playing violent video games.

The relationship between humans and animals is necessary—not for the animal but for our own sense of kinship with nature and full human development. Anatole France writes, "Until one has loved an animal a part of one's soul remains unawakened."

The function of nature is to make us closer to humanity, to understand it better, to see into its glories more deeply, to care for its pain more feelingly. "If you're going to care about the fall of the sparrow," Madeleine L'Engle writes, "you can't pick and choose who's going to be the sparrow. It's everybody."

Edith Stein brooks no doubt: To really be dedicated to God, we must be dedicated to the whole of creation. Which means the elephants in Africa, the homeless in our cities, the ice in Antarctica, and the homes built on seashores that ocean water will flood.

When we say we seek the mystical and then leave life at-large out of our collection of sacred places, we prove how profane, how secular, how truly unspiritual we really are. Ludwig Wittgenstein said once, "The mystical is not how the world is, but that it is." Ahhh, there you have it.

The important evolution is the one that happens in ourselves. This is the one that makes us aware of all life around us. Then we finally come to realize that we are simply one more part of all of it, not more than all of it.

The God of evolution is the God of growth rather than the God of law and judgment. This God allows us to learn one decision at a time and supports us as we grow into our best selves through all of them.

The major problem is: Why do we think that we can take the laws of nature and amend them till the wetlands dry up and the oceans are shed dry and the animals are slaughtered for fun? As George Bernard Shaw pointed out, we have a problem. He writes, "Human beings are the only animals of which I am thoroughly and cravenly afraid."

The problem is clear. As Ellen DeGeneres says of it, "I ask people why they have deer heads on their walls. They always say because it's such a beautiful animal. There you go! I think my mother is attractive, too, but I have photographs of her."

FOR A LISTENING HEART

*Dedication to God means dedication to the **whole** of creation.* EDITH STEIN

Spend a few minutes with this quote and then ask yourself:

- What do these words say to me? What feelings or memories do the words evoke in me?

- What do these words say about my spiritual journey?

- My journal response to this quote is:

Edith Stein (1891-1942), born into a Jewish family, be-
came an atheist as a teenager, but after earning a doctor-
ate in philosophy and reading the works of Saint Teresa of
Ávila, she converted to Catholicism and eventually joined
the Discalced Carmelite order as Teresa Benedicta of the
Cross. Refusing to leave her sister behind during the Nazi
invasion, the two were arrested and sent to their deaths
at Auschwitz. A brilliant philosopher, theologian, writer,
and lecturer, her books include **Essays on Woman.**

CHAPTER THREE

*If your steps are peaceful,
the world will have peace.*

THICH NHAT HANH

Seek Peace and Pursue It

The *Atlantic* online magazine, December 2015, cites Australian former deputy Prime Minister Tim Fischer as a fierce public critic of US gun laws. He warns people about the danger of coming to the United States, where the number of guns and amount of gun violence exceed every other country in the world. In a jibe at the NRA's claim that guns are necessary to keep the peace, Fischer argues that "if more guns made people safer, the United States would be the safest country in the world." But, truth is, we aren't.

Just reading the headlines in small-town newspapers

is enough to make the world cringe at the thought of living in the United States. "Police kill more inner-city teenagers," our papers report daily. "USA leads world in arms sales," we crow. "States legalize open carry gun proposals." And worse, according to GVA (the Gun Violence Archive begun in 2013) there were 52,073 incidents of gun violence here in 2015. Of these, 13,263 resulted in death, and 26,694 people were injured—693 of them children under the age of eleven and 2,662 of them children between the ages of twelve and seventeen. Most chilling of all, perhaps, 329 incidents of mass shootings were reported and verified.

Or to put it another way, according to *Forbes* magazine, August 2015, more young people under the age of twenty-six are now killed by guns in the United States than by cars.

Peace? What peace? "Let there be peace on earth," we sing. But we forget perhaps the rest of the hymn that counsels "and let it begin with me."

We cluck over the war zones of the world but are inclined to ignore our own. True, there is very little the average citizen can do to stop the puppet wars, the terrorist tactics, the national tensions of the world. But we could do something about our private little combats and hostilities and strife—simply by examining our own attitudes toward conflict resolution.

When winning at all costs rather than negotiating to a common satisfaction is the goal of all our internal sorties and assaults, then losing is the only other option. When the gauntlet we throw down in every conversation is: "This way and no other," we strip the other of dignity, the world of new possibilities, and ourselves of spiritual growth.

Then we set ourselves up to surrender the peace. In a situation like this, peace becomes the victim, and turmoil the environment and agitation the underlying state of our souls. It is a sad and sorry way to live. It sacrifices everything—community, success, and spiritual development—to conquest.

The price for such a false peace is devastating in itself. We silence and suppress the other, but we do not make them friends. The price for that kind of peace is simply too high for the world to long bear.

Before it's over, we will have painted ourselves out of the social picture and out of human respect. Our lives grow narrower, our friends and associates disappear, our invitations dwindle, and our hearts calcify. Peace? What kind of peace is that?

The Desert Monastics considered the question of violence, too. In one of their Sayings, they give us a clue to the way of peace. The story reads:

> There were two old men who had lived together for many years and they had never quarreled. Now one of them said: Let us try to quarrel once just like other people do. And the other replied: I don't know how a quarrel happens. Then the first one said: Look, I put a brick between us and I say, This is mine, and you say, No, it's mine, and after that a quarrel begins. So they placed a brick between them, and one of them said: This is mine, and the other said, No, it's mine. And the first replied: Indeed, it's all yours, so take it away with you! And they went away unable to fight with each other.

If we want peace in the world, we ourselves must first learn to cultivate a relaxed grasp, to bring peace as well as to want peace, to be open to new ideas, to care for the needs of the others as much as we care for our own.

The whole notion that threatening force by carrying a gun will add to the level of peace in the environment is fatuous, at best. The charade of serenity only adds tension to the tinderbox of emotions. Albert Einstein was very clear about the prospect. "Peace," he says, "cannot be kept by force; it can only be achieved by understanding."

Peace is not a factor of what's going on around us. It is a factor of what's going on within us.

The person of peace deals with turmoil out of the well of serenity, the fullness of faith, which they have spent their lives cultivating.

The serenity we bring into the room with us either enhances or diminishes the degree of serenity that is there already. "Peace," Mother Teresa says, "begins with a smile."

Do not be fooled by peace imposed by force. That kind of peace serves only to mask the underlying tensions.

———

False peace, the kind of peace that pretends there is no problem, eventually erupts. "You cannot find peace," Virginia Woolf writes, "by avoiding life." It's what we face head-on—and resolve to everyone's satisfaction— that really brings us peace.

———

To make peace with others, we must first have made peace with ourselves—with our guilt, our shame, our anger, and our hurts. Otherwise, our instinct is to expect other people to make us feel good.

———

Depending on the other to bring us peace never works for long. Either it's not good enough for you or they know it's not fair to them. "There is no path to peace," Gandhi writes. "Peace is the path."

———

To be peacemakers, we need to stop making war—with immigrants, with people unlike ourselves, with those whose ideas are uncomfortable for us.

Simply avoiding people who are different than we are does nothing to achieve peace.

We need to move toward understanding different people. The best way? Make one of them a friend and ask them to explain their beliefs, their lives, their ideas. You will be all the wiser, all the more peaceful. They will be all the more understood. As Helen Keller says, "I do not want the peace that passes understanding, I want the understanding that brings peace."

Apathy is not a substitute for peace. Apathy says, "I don't care." Peace says, "I care very much" and sets out to make it possible.

Peace is more than a lack of discord. The courage to face discord is the beginning of peace.

War is not the way to peace. It simply recruits the next generation of enemies.

Peace never lasts. It requires a constant struggle to preserve justice in situations of unequal power.

The beginning of spiritual growth requires the balance, not the elimination, of differences. To eliminate differences is to take the richness out of life.

––––––––––

Joy and peace are twins. You can't have one without the other. As Jeannette Rankin writes, "You can no more win a war than you can win an earthquake."

––––––––––

The pursuit of peace is the task of a lifetime. To abandon it is to abandon the future of the family, of the world.

––––––––––

To achieve peace on the personal level, we must be the first to give it.

––––––––––

Women make peace in the world one at a time: in the neighborhood, in the office, in the home. Isabel Allende says of a woman's place in peacemaking, "I can promise you that women working together—linked, informed, and educated—can bring peace and prosperity to this forsaken planet."

––––––––––

Don't set out to change the world. Set out to change yourself. Gerald Jampolsky says the secret lies in knowing that "peace of mind comes from not wanting to change others."

My contribution to peace must first be the cultivation of peace in me. Etty Hillesum wrote from her concentration camp, "The more peace there is in us, the more peace there will also be in our troubled world."

Just because the world around us is in turmoil—in the home, in the office, in the church—does not mean that we must necessarily be destroyed by it. Vincent van Gogh, tortured by depression, wrote, "There is peace even in the storm."

Peace requires more than the end of hostility. It demands the rebuilding of the relationship, as well.

To keep the peace means that we leave the door of our heart as well as the door of our lives forever open for the other to walk through.

Sometimes keeping the peace simply means that we have the virtue to do nothing to stir the adder's nest.

That in itself is more than enough gift to the world around us.

It's often what we do not do that is just as essential to the coming of peace as what we do. António Gutteres, former U.N. High Commissioner for Refugees, says, "Peace is not only an opportunity but an obligation."

To discover that we—ourselves, our nation, our race, our religion—are not the center of the universe is to discover the first step toward universal peace.

It is not difficult to remember that the needs of others are just as important as our own. What is difficult is to realize it. To make it real.

The war of the sexes could not exist in an environment of real equality. Catherine of Siena writes, "Wanting to live in peace is often the greatest cruelty. When the boil has come to a head, it must be cut with the lance and burned with fire, and if that is not done, and only a plaster is put on it, the corruption will spread and that is often worse than death."

When you read the next newspaper remember what Wayne Dyer writes, "Conflict cannot survive without your participation."

FOR A LISTENING HEART

If your steps are peaceful,
the world will have peace.

THICH NHAT HANH

Spend a few minutes with this quote and then ask yourself:

- What do these words say to me? What feelings or memories do the words evoke in me?

- What do these words say about my spiritual journey?

- My journal response to this quote is:

Thich Nhat Hanh is a Vietnamese Zen Master, poet, peace activist, and spiritual leader revered for his teaching and bestselling writing on mindfulness and peace. He formed Engaged Buddhism and established monasteries and sanghas globally including Plum Village in the South of France where he now lives. More information is at http:// plumvillage.org/

CHAPTER FOUR

*It is not God's fault that things are
as they are at present, but our own.*

ETTY HILLESUM

❦

Holy Accountability

Here's a quiz: What do the Adam and Eve story and the presidential election of 2016 in the United States have in common?

Give up? It's easy: free will, accountability—and oh, yes, a snake in the tree.

Adam and Eve's plight is relatively "transparent." (The current operative political word, so I used it.) They have been given a treasure. The problem that arises is whether or not the treasure has been given them to exploit for their own sakes. Or—they must figure out—is it given to them to protect, to develop, and to respect in it the face of God's glory, which is embedded there?

Which is where free will comes in. Free will—choice—is the spiritual dimension of humanity. It makes Adam and Eve responsible for doing what is best to preserve what they've been given. They are responsible for making the world better than it was before they got there. They are responsible for continuing what God created, for completing what God began, for making paradise real. Responsibility, thy name is Adam and Eve.

They are, in other words, responsible for seeing that their own behaviors do not destroy the integrity of what they've been given.

The message is clear: They are accountable for what they do. They lost "paradise," the Scripture teaches, because they ignored those responsibilities.

Even more important, as presumptive heirs of paradise, we, too, are in charge of what we've been given to protect, to develop, and to maintain in this world. And we are accountable for doing it. Otherwise, we will lose what it has taken thousands and thousands of years to develop: a habitable planet for humans, the principle of universal human rights, a place of potential and blessing for all, and, at least here, in this country, a government devoted to "life, liberty, and the pursuit of happiness"—a government of rights and responsibilities for all.

Which is where the snake, the tempter, comes in, whispering in all our ears as it did in the ears of Adam and Eve: Vote for what best expresses how you feel, how angry you are, how self-centered you are, how full of hate you are. That'll show 'em. Vote for what you want— more land, more power, more patriarchy, more exclusiveness, more control—regardless of how that would affect anyone else's sense of humanity, freedom, and equality.

No doubt about it—free will and personal responsibility are the hidden treasures of the human race. Or, as Confucius says: "Attack the evil that is within yourself, rather than attacking the evil that is in others."

No doubt about it—we are being tested on the spiritual depth of our own choices right now. And we, too, will be held accountable if, this time, it is our own whims disguised as holy choices that lose us paradise again.

The whole idea that free will is the right to choose things that benefit more than the self is a foreign one in a world of "rugged individualism." But maybe that's exactly why so much of what we call good seems sometimes to be slipping away.

It's so easy to hide behind "them," "those kind of people," "the others," when decisions go sour. The ultimate question is always a personal one, however. And it is: What did I do to support the decision-making process: Did I speak out? Did I work for the campaign I thought would do best for everyone? Did I at least vote?

To forget the gift of free will, to hide behind the choices of others because "everybody wants it," is to forgo personal power for the sake of social approval. Stanislaw Jerzy Lec writes: "No snowflake in an avalanche ever feels responsible." But that doesn't mean that it isn't.

We pray that God will save us from ourselves when actually, if we did something about what's bothering us—as God intends for us to do—that would be a miracle too.

God companions us through pain, holds us up, gives us strength. But God does not take it away. Pain is as much a part of life as is choice. It is choice—ours—that is our first antidote to pain. As Agatha Christie puts it, "There's too much tendency to attribute to God the evils that humans do of our own free will."

The great human task is to make life better for everyone. To be satisfied with anything less marks us as less than fully developed human beings.

The quality of any society depends on the integrity and commitment of its members. All the ideals in the world will not substitute for strength when strength is needed and for courage when courage is necessary. Otherwise, that population is simply a herd, not a society.

Leaders inspire a group with the kind of vision and ideals that are worth spending a life to achieve. Demagogues speak to a crowd's lowest instincts for the sake of their own aspirations to power.

What happens to the society in which we live depends

on what we ourselves are willing to do to make it better. Depending entirely on the leadership itself is what turns leaders into autocrats. Sophie Scholl writes: "How can we expect righteousness to prevail when there is hardly anyone willing to offer themselves up individually for a righteous cause?"

Demagogues live for the sound of their own voices. They believe only what they themselves think about a situation, regardless of all facts to the contrary.

To get elected, demagogues say what people want to hear, whether they have any intention—or any way—of doing it or not. They seek adulation and autocratic power.

Demagogues have a great sense of purpose and a great sense of self. The problem is that they have little or no vision broad enough to make life better for everyone they are meant to serve.

Real leaders rise above partisanship and sectarianism. Leaders know where the good of the entire group lies. Most of all, that's what they really care about.

Leaders engage talented and committed people from all perspectives on the social chart in order to see that the goals set are really meant to benefit everyone. The problem lies in finding enough people who have the same kind of holy zeal to implement them. Sigmund Freud writes: "Most people do not really want freedom because freedom involves responsibility. And most people are frightened of responsibility."

Feeling responsible for the planet changes the way we ourselves live life. It commits us to the daily things, such as saving water, recycling plastics, and reading articles on fracking and school food programs so that we can vote well.

To be responsible people in a world in transition, we don't have to do everything. But we must do some one thing, at least, that will make the future better, will make the future possible for everyone. "Each person," Voltaire writes, "is guilty of all the good they do not do."

We are, each one of us, stones skipped across the waters of the universe. The ripples of our presence, whatever it is, good or bad, radiate forever. As you go, in other words, so goes the world. Now tell me again, what is it in life that you want someone else to correct?

———

Nothing the world needs now can possibly be accomplished overnight. But if we do not each begin to do our part today, it will never, ever come.

———

What we do nothing to prevent today may well come tomorrow. Just when we aren't looking. As Molière writes, "It is not only what we do, but also what we do not do, for which we are accountable."

———

The herd mentality says that I will go where the crowd goes because they know better than I do. The Christian mentality says that I will do as Jesus did because that is the will of God for me.

———

Nothing worth doing can be done quickly. It takes days of the giving of the self. It takes a lifetime of doing what may not seem to work. But as the Zen master says, "No seed ever sees the flower."

There is only one way to a better tomorrow. And that lies in getting up every day, every year, for an entire life-time intent on going one more step in that direction. As Catherine of Siena wrote centuries ago: "Nothing great is ever achieved without much enduring."

In every election, our own personal, individual responsibility is to ask ourselves exactly why I am voting for the candidate of my choice. Is it to quell my own anger and frustration? Is my vote intended to exclude others? Is my vote meant to enhance my own position at the expense of innocent others? The fact is, why I vote for someone is every bit as important as the candidate I choose.

If only I knew how important I am. If I ever really understood how what I think and say affects other people, it would change my sense of self. I would begin to realize how much of what I do—or do not do—really matters to the future.

How is it that we always think that what must be done will be done by someone else? Then, when it isn't, whom do we blame? Frederick Douglass has the answer.

He writes: "I prayed for twenty years but received no answer until I prayed with my legs."

―――――――

Being quiet in the midst of turmoil does nothing to solve the problem. It only increases my need to excuse my indifference, my cowardliness, by pretending that I'm simply trying not to add to the uproar. Or as Maya Angelou says: "People will judge you by your actions, not your intentions. You may have a heart of gold but so does a hard-boiled egg."

―――――――

Listen to yourself carefully. Are you in the practice of giving excuses to explain your absence from public concerns? As in, "I was busy" or "I didn't know about the meeting" or "I don't know how to contact any of these people." Really? Or is the real answer: Fear? Indifference? Disengagement from the human enterprise? Saint Augustine says of situations like this: "God provides the wind but the individual must raise the sails."

―――――――

The world is waiting to find out what you think about a thing—and why. Do you know? If not, remember that to think and do nothing to discover where you stand on the important questions of life is also harmful.

———————

To those who say to themselves, "There's nothing I can do about it," Joan of Arc had an answer. She said: "Act, and God will act."

———————

"In dreams begins responsibility," William Butler Yeats writes. The vernacular of that may not be poetic but it is surely clear: Don't sit around wishing something would happen. Gather the people who can help you and see that it gets done.

———————

The words of Franklin Delano Roosevelt may well have been written for these times. He warns us: "True individual freedom cannot exist without economic security and independence. People who are hungry and out of a job are the stuff of which dictatorships are made."

*It is not God's fault that things are
as they are at present, but our own.*
ETTY HILLESUM

Spend a few minutes with this quote and then ask
yourself:

- What do these words say to me? What feelings or
  memories do the words evoke in me?

- What do these words say about my spiritual journey?

- My journal response to this quote is:

_____

Etty Hillesum was an extraordinary young Jewish woman from Amsterdam who lived between 1914 and 1943. She kept many diaries and journals describing life under Nazi occupation, as well as her own inward, spiritual journey. She discovered that she lived in "constant intimacy with God." She died in Auschwitz, at the age of 29. Her diaries and letters, An Interrupted Life, *were first published in 1981.*

CHAPTER FIVE

*If you want others to be happy,
practice compassion. If you want
to be happy, practice compassion.*

DALAI LAMA

To Be Truly Human

I've written or spoken a good many times about the incivility that unmonitored social media sites have generated in this country. Someplace along the line we have managed to confuse freedom of speech with the freedom to be rude, crude, mean, hurtful, or brutal—anonymously. Secretly. Behind some silly moniker like "Darth Vader 2." Or worse.

I grew up in a society where there were some words that were never spoken—in front of women, in front of children, in public, at a dinner table, in a professional setting, on a telecommunications program of any kind. But then little by little, we began to see it painted on back walls of old buildings. And did nothing. Then we began to accept it in teenage music. And did nothing. Then it showed up in racy "literature." And we did nothing. Finally, it was everywhere. And now, it seems, there is very little we can do about it at all.

Where did we lose the idea that freedom of speech is the right to have our speech protected, no matter what our opinion might be? That does not, however, include the right to libel, slander, and now bully people into submission. It does not include a license to abuse someone—meaning to call names or threaten harm or talk or harass those who are different than we are. Physically, socially, or politically. There are statutes against it. So much for the law. So much for our birthright. So much for the character of the nation. So much for our vaunted ideals of democracy.

Obviously, given the increase in the amount of outright lies or veiled insults in the public airwaves now, the threat of the law does not really much restrain an anonymous population, let alone educate it to a more civilized kind of communication. Those websites that employ monitors with the right to reject that level of so-called "comments" manage to maintain a higher standard of conversation and insight. But for smaller groups with fewer resources, the ability to engage that kind of monitor is more likely to threaten the existence of the website itself than it is to eliminate the problem.

And so we all know that. And so we don't know what to do about it. Except maybe inspect our own children's websites in the hope of being able to separate them from the adults around them who are even more childish, more crude, than the average adolescent.

But now we have struck a new low. A gutter talk so bad that we don't want children even to watch the news. Now it's our national leaders who are leading the pack. These valiant types who purport to be the role models of the country. These high-level poobahs who speak from the Olympian Heights of business, politics, and public service have long ago sliced and diced not only one another but the character of the country itself.

I am in Europe as I write this, where the attitude about what they are seeing of us on television is clear but said in far more elegant, more honest, more caring language than ours for one another. They feel sorry for us. They wonder what is happening to those decent rank and file citizens, real Christians, genuine intellectuals, committed activists, genuine patriots who are embarrassed by their own political parties.

And we, for our part, ask ourselves what has happened to us. How has compassion—the ability to really feel for the other, to care for the other as well as ourselves, to be different than others but never destructive of others—disappeared?

Maybe compassion here and now calls for us to quench this fire at its lowest level—on our comment boards, in our blogs, in our texts, in our chat rooms. To refuse to read them. To "unlike" all of them. Then, eventually, it can become unacceptable again to use that kind of language anywhere. Even in our presidential elections. At the top.

So now we're split as a country, as a body politic, as a generation. Why? Because we ignored this malignancy and let it spread. Has it helped us express ourselves? Has it helped us to make our points any better, any more effectively? Has it brought us to the point of effective political discourse? Has it made us any happier? The Dalai Lama's statement says it all: "If you want others to be happy, practice compassion. If you want to be happy, practice compassion."

From where I stand, it seems to me that to be compassionate in this environment, we can't say "It's awful" anymore. We need to say "It stops here. In front of me. Always."

When we forget to be kind, we forget what it is to be human, to be able to determine both our feelings and our actions. Then we abandon responsibility, yes. But more than that, we relinquish our own right to be loved.

The ability to understand the feelings of another increases the level of human bonding, national bonding everywhere.

There can never be too much kindness in life—either for us or because of us. Every act of kindness makes the world a softer, better place. As Aesop writes, "No act of kindness, no matter how small, is ever wasted."

Kindness is not about being right or just or strong. It is about being determined not to add to the suffering of the world. Which means that being kind to those who some would say do not deserve our kindness may do more to change the world than being just will ever do.

What people need most after they have made a mistake is not correction. It is kindness. "Compassion," Henry Ward Beecher writes, "will cure more sins than condemnation."

We must be kind to ourselves as well as to others. Otherwise, how will we ever find the resources within us to go out of our way to be kind to others? The Buddha says, "If your compassion does not include yourself, it is incomplete."

When we are rigid with ourselves, we give ourselves the right to be even more rigid with others. Or to put it another way: All spirit comes from the top. Mother Teresa writes, "I would rather make mistakes in kindness and compassion than work miracles in unkindness and hardness."

Compassion is what enables us to help one another through life, the only goal really worth giving our lives to making real.

Every pain we ourselves suffer seeds the possibility that we can come out of struggle softer, more tender, than ever before. The poet Rumi writes of it, "You have to keep breaking your heart until it opens."

Kindness is not weakness. It demonstrates superhuman strength to take the broken and the beaten into our arms until they are capable of standing alone. "Compassion," Frederick Buechner writes, "is the knowledge that there can never really be any peace and joy for me until there is peace and joy finally for you, too."

Everything we do or do not do for another either raises or lowers the degree of humanity in the world. We can sit around and bemoan the level of kindness everywhere, but nothing changes until we ourselves do more to raise it.

No wars would ever start, no bombs would ever fall, if compassion, rather than fear, were the DNA of society.

In order to reach out to an enemy, we must first seek to understand what it is that is making the other our enemy. Only then are we able to step across the threshold of the other with the kind of understanding that gives rise to both compassion and cooperation.

Compassion and charity are not the same things—though one may lead to the other. Charity sees a need and fills it. Dorothy Day says that "charity is only as warm as those who administer it."

Compassionate people see suffering and feel it to such a degree that they themselves become part of the struggle until the suffering ends.

Charity is reserved for the other, the ones not like us. Compassion arises out of the awareness that those who suffer are simply the other side of ourselves. They remind us of our own vulnerability and the fact that someday we will suffer too. Then what? "The whole idea of compassion," Thomas Merton says, "is based on a keen awareness of the interdependence of all these living beings, which are all part of one another, and all involved in one another."

The harshness with which we judge the other will some day be the measure by which we ourselves are judged. "I really only love God," Dorothy Day writes, "as much as I love the person I love the least."

What we all depend on is the compassion of God. My eternal spiritual question must therefore be: Who is depending on me for the same thing?

According to the Max Planck Institute in Germany, on the topic of compassion, belief is not what shapes us. What shapes us is action. The point is that to be what we say we are, we must do compassion until we become it.

Compassion is not sympathy, it is empathy. Sympathy understands the feelings of the one who suffers; empathy feels the feelings of those who are suffering. And Daniel Goleman goes even further. He writes, "True compassion means not only feeling another's pain but also being moved to help relieve it."

Nothing will change about the levels of national homelessness, for instance, until those who are not homeless allow themselves to feel what it would be like to wake up every day knowing you do not have money for rent. Maybe if the rest of the country slept in their cars with their children one night, we could get the problem solved more quickly. Compassion is so much faster than legislation.

Compassion is based on love for the unknown other. Anne Lamott says, "If you love, you will grieve." Which means, of course, that we will do whatever is needed to save them from pain.

Compassion saves us from going through life soulless—unaware of anyone but ourselves. George Bernard Shaw writes of it, "The worst sin toward our fellow creatures is not to hate them, but to be indifferent to them: that's the essence of inhumanity."

The compassionate person does not sit in front of the TV and weep. They do something, however small, to take the suffering away.

Compassion is gentle, is kind. To be gentle is, first, to be soft of speech. Soft enough to be able to hear the words of the other rather than attempt to suppress their concerns by overtalking them.

To be truly human, we cannot simply regret the massive suffering of the thousands literally dying in a last great effort to live. We must become the suffering ourselves. Then, and not until then, when we ourselves call to politicians everywhere, will such wholesale suffering stop.

Compassion does not question, does not judge, does not lecture. Compassion concentrates on healing the pain. Henri Nouwen puts it best: "When we honestly ask ourselves which person in our lives meant the most to us, we often find that it is those who, instead of giving advice, solutions, or cures, have chosen rather to share our pain and touch our wounds with a warm and tender hand."

The major question in life is: What kind of a person do I want to be? And then, I must begin to be what I want to be. "Accustom yourself continually," Teresa of Ávila says, "to making many acts of love, for they enkindle and melt the soul."

It is easy to talk about compassion. Most people do. But to understand the difference between compassion and run-of-the-mill kindness can take a while. The moral problem is that we are inclined to wait till we're sure what it means. Thomas Aquinas, one of the greatest thinkers of all time, gave up on the question. He wrote, "I would rather feel compassion than know the meaning of it." Good idea.

Compassion is the practice of unconditional love. Unconditional. Oh.

We have two choices: compassion or revenge. Choose. "When," Eleanor Roosevelt asks, "will our consciences grow so tender that we will act to prevent human misery rather than avenge it?" Perhaps that is the one question that needs to be answered in this period of Great

Migration when toddlers sleep in wet tents or walk miles to find gates closed everywhere.

FOR A LISTENING HEART

If you want others to be happy, practice compassion. If you want to be happy, practice compassion.

DALAI LAMA

Spend a few minutes with this quote and then ask yourself:

- What do these words say to me? What feelings or memories do the words evoke in me?

- What do these words say about my spiritual journey?

- My journal response to this quote is:

The Fourteenth Dalai Lama, (born 1935) Tenzin Gyatso, is the spiritual leader of Tibet, believed by Buddhists to be a reincarnation of the Bodhisattva of Compassion. A Buddhist monk since early childhood, he is an advocate for nonviolence, even in the face of persecution, and for environmentalism. He has been awarded the Nobel Peace Prize, held interfaith dialogues, and published over 110 books.

CHAPTER SIX

Cry out with a thousand tongues.
I see the world is rotten because of silence.

St. Catherine of Siena

Breaking the Silence

After the Kitty Genovese murder case in 1964, social psychologists everywhere concentrated on answering the question that plagued not only the people of New York but people across the country as well. One after another they asked themselves: How is it that anywhere from twelve people to over twice that number could have heard, even seen, some parts of the attack and yet done nothing to save her?

Bleeding to death from three separate knife attacks, Genovese's cries for help to the people in her own apartment building went unanswered. Despite the fact that many admitted to hearing the cries and even seeing a scuffle.

Only after the attack had ended and the cries went silent did one woman appear to check her wounds and one man called the police. She died a full thirty minutes after the attack began—in the ambulance on the way to the hospital. If help had been summoned sooner, where would she be now?

The questions touch the depth of the human soul: What can possibly account for such unconcern? For such apathy? Is it the anonymity factor of large cities? As in, I don't know the person, so I don't do anything? Is it the diffusion factor that comes with large groups? As in, I'm sure some of all these other people will do something so I don't need to. Is it driven by pure self-centeredness? As in, it's not my problem and I don't want to get involved.

So, whatever the reason I give myself for ignoring someone else's crisis, I simply ignore what's happening in front of my face and go my self-centered, self-protective way.

Maybe we're at a point in a society high on individualism that we are now reaping what we have planted: a general lack of personal care, a dearth of commitment to the common good, a shortage of personal responsibility in a world full of nameless, faceless people to whom we have no attachments and in whom we take no interest.

In a society of strangers, in a world where rural villagers are now more the rarity than the norm, we all live private lives in increasingly larger groups where no one is responsible and everyone is responsible at the same time.

But the great saints allow for no such excuses. They confront us with being keepers of the Garden wherever we are. Wherever we are, they show us, justice must reign, equality must prevail, and the defense of the little ones of God must be assured. By us.

Catherine of Siena is clear about the implications of it. When anything deviates from the will of God, we must leap to the bar to defend those on whom the burden will fall most heavily, most urgently, most unfairly. We must carry on our own shoulders our weakest as well as our strong.

"Cry out with a thousand tongues," Catherine of Siena writes. "I see the world is rotten because of silence."

It is your voice and mine, alone as well as together,

that are meant to raise the alarms. If we don't point out the breakdowns in human community and make clear the unseen millions in need, they go on being unseen by the many.

Perhaps the clearest words of moral instruction written in our own times are not in the Bible. They come from Pastor Martin Niemöller during World War II. He wrote:

> First they came for the Communists, and I did not
>   speak out, because I was not a Communist.
> Then they came for the Socialists, and I did not
>   speak out, because I was not a Socialist.
> Then they came for the trade unionists, and I did not
>   speak out, because I was not a trade unionist.
> Then they came for the Jews, and I did not
>   speak out, because I was not a Jew.
> Then they came for me, and there was no one left
>   to speak out for me.

There is someone right now, right here, who is crying out for help. Whose voice are you not listening to today?

As more and more cries out to be done in this country as well as abroad, it is so easy to simply forget all of it. "I can't do a thing about any of it," we say. And so we don't. And so it all goes on. Helen Keller wrote once: "Science may have found a cure for most evils; but it has found no remedy for the worst of them all—the apathy of human beings."

Evil can only remain evil as long as the rest of the world continues to be silent about it.

It is not a matter of being able to change a thing that must occupy us. It is a matter of being willing to point out the problem—and do something—that counts. "How wonderful it is," Anne Frank writes, "that nobody need wait a single moment before starting to improve the world."

When I am unconcerned about the issues of the world, the plans and programs and principles that affect the lives of thousands, I am already dead. At least in soul.

To complain about public policies is not enough. Change requires that we be willing to stand up for something. And most of all, we must be willing to pay the social price that comes with taking a stand in public.

It's easy to become accustomed to injustice. What is really difficult is to do something about stopping it.

To change a policy or practice, join a group that is committed to the same issue. Then, with everyone else, push. As Joe Hill says, "Don't mourn; organize."

Our problem is that we expect change to come in our lifetime. But until we ourselves begin to work for change, nothing can ever happen. Our task is to prepare for its coming, not necessarily to ever enjoy it ourselves.

Change is obstructed by apathy—and by fear. Apathy requires that we confront ourselves. Fear requires that we challenge our opposition. Allan Boesak says of change, "We will go before God to be judged and God will ask us, 'Where are your wounds?' And we will say,

'We have no wounds.' And God will ask, 'Was nothing worth fighting for?'"

The most effective chains are the ones with which we bind ourselves. And why would we do that? Because being bound is more comfortable than the task of having to face what it will take to break them ourselves.

No, it's not possible to do everything ourselves. But who cares? What's important is that it gets done. Whatever support we can give others who are doing it, the easier it is for them to go on. As Henry Adams says, paraphrasing Milton, "They too serve a certain purpose who only stand and cheer!"

To be part of a group intent on change, we will raise a great voice, make a long shadow, and, together, build a new picture of possibility. It doesn't matter how great a task we do; licking envelopes or handing out posters will do it.

Sympathy is no substitute for action. The question is: What did I do today to minimize the evil in the world, in my neighborhood, in my family? Allen Ginsburg says of it, "It isn't enough for your heart to break, because everybody's heart is broken now."

The great trick is to remember to "cry out" to the right people—overlords, civil or religious—and in the right way, clearly but nonviolently. Most of all, we must "cry out" as long as it takes. One email does not a movement make. "For evil to succeed," Edmund Burke wrote, "all it needs is for good people to do nothing."

In order to change things, we must all begin to live our lives, as Dorothy Day says, "in drastically different ways." By speaking up, and speaking out, and speaking on.

It is easy to forgive ourselves for doing nothing. "I don't know anything about that," we say. But Murray Cohen answers us back: "The ark was built by amateurs and the Titanic by experts. Don't wait for the experts."

Our problem is not that we can't correct the errors of society. Our problem is that we let them happen in the first place: like grinding poverty, climate change, sexism, and social exclusionism. Until we each take serious steps daily to combat these social diseases, we shall each remain responsible for their growth.

When we cleanse our own lives of social exclusion and discrimination we make the whole world a better place. "When will our consciences grow so tender," Eleanor Roosevelt asked, "that we will act to prevent human misery rather than avenge it?"

To "cry out" is to risk being socially excluded ourselves. But it is, at the same time, a guarantee of social consciousness, your gift to the next generation. As Isadora Duncan says, "Don't let them tame you!"

We may not see much change in our lifetime but before we go we can at least salt the atmosphere with questions where they cannot be ignored. And that is valor enough for the moment.

Silence is a virtue only when it prepares us to act well later. Otherwise, it runs the risk of becoming nothing more than a symptom of spiritual narcissism.

Real concern does not depress us. What good is the ability to recognize unnecessary pain if we become its next victim? Instead, real concern focuses our mind; it sharpens our hearts; it becomes the fuel of change. "Concern," Karen Horney says, "should drive us into action, not into depression."

There is no such thing as "neutrality" in the face of evil. Not to make a decision is a decision. We decide to cooperate with evil by doing nothing to stop it. Bishop Desmond Tutu explains it this way: "If an elephant has its foot on the tail of a mouse and you say that you are neutral, the mouse will not appreciate your neutrality."

To reach out a steadying hand, an open heart, a mind for understanding the griefs and losses and mistakes of the other, makes our own lives more valuable. Then, the world needs us. To be able to feel with the other makes us useful to the world.

We cannot cure any situation, personal or social, until we understand it. When we begin to understand not only what is happening but why it is happening, we are ready now to help make the world a better place.

No one "belongs" to a group—either an organization or a country—if they do not take responsibility for forming its decisions and then protecting them. As Charles de Montesquieu says, "The tyranny of a prince in an oligarchy is not so dangerous to the public welfare as the apathy of a citizen in a democracy."

Don't be afraid to get involved. Being uninvolved when involvement is clearly needed is a far greater error than is trying and failing.

When we try to eradicate evil but fail, goodness wins nevertheless because trying keeps the hope of goodness alive.

To tolerate evil is to make friends with it, to allow it in and make it welcome, to give it a place at the table. James Goldsmith says of it, "Tolerance is a tremendous virtue but the immediate neighbors of tolerance are apathy and weakness."

Those who stand for nothing have never really lived.

~~~~~~~~~~~~~~~~~~~~~~~~~~~~~~~~~~~~

Anthony de Mello tells a story about apathy: A young man eagerly described what he dreamed of doing for the poor. Said the master, "When do you propose to make your dream come true?" The young man answered, "As soon as opportunity arrives." "Opportunity never arrives," said the master. "It's here." "Cry out" and turn now into the moment of opportunity for many.

Cry out with a thousand tongues.
I see the world is rotten because of silence.

ST. CATHERINE OF SIENA

Spend a few minutes with this quote and then ask yourself:

- What do these words say to me? What feelings or memories do the words evoke in me?

- What do these words say about my spiritual journey?

- My journal response to this quote is:

Saint Catherine of Siena (1347-1380), was a Dominican often credited, through the influence of her letters, with returning the papacy of Gregory XI to Rome after its exile to Avignon. She brokered peace between Florence and Rome, and at the request of Pope Urban VI travelled to Rome to stabilize the papacy once again. She is one of the Doctors of the Church, and co-patron of Italy with Saint Francis of Assisi.

CHAPTER SEVEN

*We are not human beings having
a spiritual experience. We are spiritual
beings having a human experience.*

PIERRE TEILHARD DE CHARDIN

Sparks of the Divine

L ife without a purpose equal to the greatness that comes simply from being human is life without meaning. Worse, it is life in danger of despair. After all, why go through all the effort, all the sacrifice, all the uncertainty that comes with simply being alive when there is nothing for which all the struggle is worth?

It is the question that lurks in the shadows of every major dimension of life. Why go on with the marriage when going on gets difficult unless something greater than the self is at stake?

Why go on with public service when what we strive for never comes?

Why go on working hard when the work seems to get us nowhere and never really succeeds, if by success we mean it never really pays off in terms of money and comfort, security and status, pride and profit?

Why keep trying to turn swords into plowshares in one of the most militarized countries in the history of the world while the poor stay poor, and the once civilized cities deteriorate, and human dignity disappears with low-wage jobs?

The questions—all of them honest, all of them important, all of them true—go on forever, in even the most developed parts of the world.

What is it that keeps us trying to make the country better and life more human for everyone in a world that tips and tilts precariously between human dignity and human degradation? What keeps us intent on human community when our own relationships end or shrivel or die?

What is it that drives us to keep straining up the hills of our lives in the face of failure after failure?

It is the deep-down soulful awareness that there is

more to this life than simply life itself. There is more to be gotten by being fully alive than simply the thought of staying alive.

In fact, if truth were known, it is not what is outside of us for which most of us struggle. On the contrary, we live on, move on, wrestle through dailiness from childhood to old age, not to arrive but to go on becoming. It is the more of life that seduces us to live fully, not the things of life that entice us.

If anything, we live the first third of life blissfully unaware of anything but its basics—good friends, good fun, good food, a good future. It's in the second third of life that we develop a taste for the best contacts, the most exotic experiences, the choicest menus, and an unbounded future. It's in the final period—the movement of life toward its end, when everything has been gained—that we really begin to be aware that life has not been much about life at all. It has only been about learning to live well. It is learning to live to our inmost limits, to live in a way that we become the best we can possibly be, that makes us aware of the real value of life.

It's then that we begin to understand that life has been more about the shaping of the spirit than it has been the accumulation of things. It's then that we finally come to know that it has been about our inner selves—our generous souls, our happy hearts, our loving relationships, our worthwhile work, successful or not—rather than our public status, that life has been about all along.

It's true that "we can't take it with us." It is also true that we have been made to become all that becoming is worth. Then, we discover, that we have really become everything that life can give us.

Clearly, as Chardin says, "We are not human beings having a spiritual experience; we are spiritual beings having a human experience."

It is, in the end, who and what we have become spiritually in life that finally, ultimately, counts.

The reason no amount of things ever really satisfies us is because we are not completed as human beings by the number of things we accumulate in life. The human being is only satisfied by growing to full stature spiritually.

It's when we grow inwardly that what we have become outwardly begins to mean less and less. Then becoming the kind of person we are meant to be is what measures the quality of our humanity.

We are all born unfinished. Then the way we deal with life is what really finishes us. It's that finished self that we give back to God. As the theologian Hans Urs von Balthasar writes, "What you are is God's gift to you; what you become is your gift to God."

All of life, everything in the universe, is made almost entirely from the same four elements—carbon, hydrogen, oxygen, and nitrogen. All of life comes from the same source and out of the same components. It is impossible to divide life into the spiritual and the material as if they were two different things.

Creation is clear: all of matter is spiritual and all that is spiritual comes to us in the material. As Henri Nouwen puts it, "The spiritual life does not remove us from the world but leads us deeper into it."

When we call part of life "only matter" and, therefore, call matter unimportant, we close ourselves off from the deepest spiritual lessons there are. We call eliminating poverty "unimportant," for instance, because the afterlife will be better, and fail to realize that the reason for destitution on earth is the undeveloped spirit in the rest of us.

―――――――――――――

God made both us and the stars out of the same material. There is, then, no difference between spirit and flesh. We are simply stardust on our way back to the source of life.

―――――――――――――

Our spiritual souls are formed by the way we treat matter. There is no holiness whatsoever that arises out of spiritual exercises alone.

―――――――――――――

Made from the universal stuff of creation, we are not totally independent, never completely unique, not alone in our humanity. The theologian Paul Tillich writes, "The most intimate motions within the depths of our souls are not completely our own. For they belong also to our friends, to humankind, to the universe, and the Ground of all being, the aim of our life."

There is a universal knowing in us that we are not a being unto ourselves. We have come from somewhere and are on the way back to it. We are each of the essence of life and cannot be whole until we are as much spiritual as we are material.

The soul of a person is the heart of the Divine given us to make the world in which we live a holier, happier place. We become co-creators with God.

When we do not examine the soul-life within us, we go through life as empty shells attempting to be filled by what itself lacks Spirit—money, possessions, power, privilege.

The body grows faster than the soul, true, but without the soul, the body never grows to the fullness of itself at all.

Only by going down into our own souls are we able to hear the Divine that resides within us. Sue Monk Kidd writes, "I eventually found that the soul is more than an immortal commodity to win and save. It is the repository of the inner divine, the truest part of us."

The restlessness within us is the spirit of Life trying to grow beyond what we see to the depths of what, innately, we already know: There is much more to life than this.

The voice of God speaks to us from within as well as from outside of us. It is in learning to listen to the Voice within that we really come to understand our place in the world. A.R. Rahman writes, "Your inner voice is the voice of divinity. To hear it, we need to be in solitude, even in crowded places."

There is a gift of the soul within each of us that is meant to be developed for the sake of the rest of the world. Bruce Barton writes, "If you have anything really valuable to contribute to the world it will come through the expression of your own personality, that single part of divinity that sets you off and makes you different from every other living creature."

Because we cannot see the soul, we are inclined to discount it—despite the fact that we each know that within us is the fire, the energy, and the value that is ours alone. It is precisely this that makes us each a singular spark of the Divine. Pope Francis is clear. He teaches, "A spark of divine light is within each of us."

It is the Spirit in us and the Spirit in the universe that is incorruptible; it is the energy of eternal life.

It is obvious that the physical part of us must be nourished into growth. What we fail to understand with equal certainty is that the soul itself, unquenchable spirit, must also be nourished, be shaped, and be allowed to come to fullness.

To fail to nourish the spiritual dimensions of life within us is to go through life bereft of its eternal values, its everlasting beauty, its overarching truths, its deepest sensitivities. It is possible, in other words, to be a body that is sterile of soul.

The soul must be trained like the eye to see the rest of life, like the ear to hear the real music of life, like the heart to beat for things worth saving. "The spark divine dwells in thee," Ella Wheeler Wilcox, American author and poet, writes. "Let it grow."

The divinity of Spirit that we have within us is here to finish the Creation that the Divine Spirit began.

Everybody's soul is another sliver of the Divine. "Your soul," T.F. Hodge writes, "is God's imagination."

It is the part of us that is soul, that trace of Divinity on earth, that will in the end melt back into God.

The soul is the magnet within that draws us out of ourselves to go on creating even greater things that enhance life for everyone. "The incredible process of being human," Lena Lee writes, "allows for the higher self to acknowledge and extract divinity from one's trials and tribulations."

To assume that catering to the body is enough to make a human being wholly human completely overlooks what it is that makes us human in the first place.

It's not enough to live through the body only. It's imperative to bring the soul to the joys, the excitement, the goals of life or what we finally gain will be a hollow attempt at life. Only if we relish what we do and do it with a purpose beyond itself can we make every moment of life count for more than our own satisfaction.

 To recognize the presence of the soul in everyone is to open the road to global peace. Maya Angelou says of it, "While I know myself as a creation of God, I am also obligated to realize and remember that everyone else and everything else are also God's creation."

The soul is what makes us children of God and not just another animal emerging from the slime. Pope Shenouda III of Alexandria teaches, "The world sees in our conduct, in our behavior, the proof that we are the real children of God."

The human soul is what gives us the right, the responsibility, to stretch ourselves to the utmost. In us is the presence of God on earth. Evelyn Underhill writes, "There is no place in my soul, no corner of my character, where God is not."

FOR A LISTENING HEART

We are not human beings having a spiritual experience. We are spiritual beings having a human experience.

PIERRE TEILHARD DE CHARDIN

Spend a few minutes with this quote and then ask yourself:

- What do these words say to me? What feelings or memories do the words evoke in me?

- What do these words say about my spiritual journey?

- My journal response to this quote is:

Pierre Teilhard de Chardin (1881-1955) was a Jesuit priest, paleontologist, geologist, and philosopher. He worked on developing a view of an evolving universe that interwove science and spiritual consciousness. His best-known works are The Phenomenon of Man *and* The Divine Milieu.

*Everything ripens at its time
and becomes fruit at its hour.*

DIVYAVADANA

Life Is a Ripening Process

Divyavadana's lovely thought that "Everything ripens at its time and becomes fruit at its hour" is exactly that—a lovely thought. If only we believed it.

Agricultural societies whose life was spent watching seeds come to ripe had a much better chance of understanding a statement like that than we do. They might even appreciate it. We don't.

In our society and in this generation—only about twenty-five years after the popular use of the internet began—life doesn't slow cook. It's on microwave at all times. We don't know what it is to wait for radishes to ripen anymore. We buy them in January in supermarkets that buy them from hothouses a world away from us. What's important is that they get them to us, this generation thinks. Not that somebody stands by for half their lives just waiting for them to grow.

Instead, we push growth—both the radishes and our own. We have hurry-up chemicals to sprinkle on our gardens and year-round imports to slake the thirst of early harvests. More than that, we want to live life in the fast lane too: We come out of school half-baked and despair for want of management jobs and management salaries. We buy a starter house but want the swimming pool and guest rooms to go with it. We want to retire early and travel.

We want to push life to its edge, and we despair when it grows at a slower pace than we would like. But life is not lived on a calendar of plans. It is lived in stages of surprise. We get exactly what we do not want until we have learned to take what life has to give.

Life comes when we're ready for it, when we can appreciate it best, when we're ready for its responsibilities. Not as our whim and fancy demands.

We want success—meaning achievement—before we are ready to take the blows or do the work that comes with it. Success comes when it is no longer a substitute for our real self.

We want security before we've earned it. But security doesn't come until security is not our only value in life.

We want love before we're wise enough to know that love comes in exact proportion to what we're willing to give of it ourselves.

Life is a ripening process. Like avocados, we look a lot better on the outside than we've become on the inside, and we so often confuse the two. Which, of course, is so often the reason that when we do finally get the fancy job, it does not satisfy. We are simply not ready to understand it or our inner selves. So we live on appearance for a long time before we're ready for the real thing.

But there comes a time, a moment, in which everything changes and we hardly ever know why. We hear people in every category talk about how hard they worked for years—but nothing ever came of it. No money. No attention. No down deep sense of freedom and joy in it. Just work and rejection and a feeling of failure.

And then, suddenly, when we need it less, it all begins to happen—almost without us, it seems.

The children come back home as adults and the relationship between us flowers.

The employer we thought did not know our name suddenly promotes us to the position we always wanted.

For no apparent reason at all, being at home takes on an aura of completeness. Despite the loss of excitement and the social whirlwind, we're happy. We're grown up emotionally and settled down professionally. We're happy. Really happy for a change.

We all grow to the fullness of our aspirations but hardly ever at the pace of the calendar we planned for them. Instead, life has other things to offer us: work, human development, wisdom. And those things come only after we have given ourselves, heart and soul, to the humdrum and the dullness of life. Then we're ready and cannot be corrupted by the empty seductions of it.

The gardeners are right: when we're ripe, we'll blossom. The real wisdom is to be patient with the ripening which, in the end, brings out the best in us however trying the tests of the seasons.

Time is as necessary to human development as it is to the development of nature. Time cannot be rushed but it can be trusted.

As we grow we change, we bloom, we soften to the world around us.

It is natural to grow but it is challenging at every stage. It stretches us when we would most prefer to be allowed to let everybody else do the heavy lifting in life.

Development is about responsibility. What will I do today? must not be permitted to be simply a personal question. The world is expecting each of us to do something that makes it better.

We exhaust ourselves running from one useless task to another. We live in a revolving door of speed for its own sake. In the midst of a changing world, as Gail Sheehy says, "speed helps people think they are keeping up."

The problem is not change. The problem is that we too easily get accustomed to doing nothing of public value. Then, the very center of the society around us begins to decay.

—————

Change for the sake of change stands to abort the process of natural growth—in both soul and body. We leap from one thing to another, learning little along the way either about the world around us or our own responsibility to it.

—————

To refuse to grow is to remain a child forever. And some people do. But when we fail to grow from one struggle to another we shrink the wisdom each stage is meant to bring.

—————

Human growth is not even. One part of us thrives; another part of us lags behind. Often, for instance, we grow in vision but not in tolerance. It is the discomfort of that kind of imbalance that requires us to keep on growing.

—————

Human growth is subtle. Often we do not know we have grown in one way until challenged in another. George

Eliot says of that process, "Our consciousness rarely registers the beginning of a growth within us any more than without us: there have been many circulations of the sap before we detect the smallest sign of the bud."

We can change ourselves to fit the style of life around us. But then, where do we go to find our real selves?

We grow up. We do not always grow better or deeper or kinder or sweeter. It all depends on how we respond along the way. As Louisa May Alcott writes: "But buds will be roses, and kittens, cats. More's the pity."

There is no such thing as non-growth. Growth is of the nature of life. Helen Hoover explains it this way: "The natural world is dynamic. From the expanding universe to the hair on a baby's head, nothing is the same from now to the next moment." Which is why, of course, that we all deserve a second chance.

To know if we're getting better as we go, all we need to do is ask ourselves whether I handled today's irritation better than I handled it yesterday.

101

Change and growth are not the same thing. Just because we change is no guarantee that we have become a better human being as a result.

A society that is not devoted to the development of all the gifts of all the people is a society in decline. It won't be long until it runs out of exactly what it needs to be great. Albert Einstein writes: "All that is valuable in human society depends upon the opportunity for development accorded the individual."

The society that leaves women out of the process of development at every and any level is a society that has doomed itself to mediocrity. It is a society in need of change—for its own sake. As Elizabeth Blackwell writes: "If society will not admit of woman's free development, then society must be remodeled." And we are still a long way away from that.

Stubbornness is no synonym for consistency. It simply means that faced with challenge we retreat into a safer past.

To live a full and productive life we must be willing to begin over and over again. As Bernie Siegel puts it: "God wants us to know that life is a series of beginnings, not endings. Just as graduations are not terminations but commencements."

The movement from one stage of life to another is never easy. It requires that we leave behind what we know and venture into a new and demanding darkness. But unless we are willing to move on, what we have learned in the past will not be enough to enable us to survive the future.

By the end of life, all the changes of life we have survived successfully will bring us to the point of emotional invincibility. As Max Lerner says, "The turning point in the process of growing up is when you discover the core of strength within you that survives all hurt."

The purpose of life is not stability of outlook, changelessness of attitude, or commitment to rigidity. The purpose of life is transformation.

No one else shapes us. We shape ourselves. We are responsible for one thing above all: the attitudes we bring to every challenge in which we find ourselves.

⌇⌇⌇⌇⌇⌇⌇⌇⌇⌇⌇⌇⌇⌇⌇⌇⌇⌇

There is no way to stop change and challenge. It is, however, possible to refuse to deal with them. And that, of course, is the definition of the death of the soul.

⌇⌇⌇⌇⌇⌇⌇⌇⌇⌇⌇⌇⌇⌇⌇⌇⌇⌇

The commitment to growth says always, "What did I learn from that situation?" Anything else is to plunge headlong from one bad situation to another equally destructive one. And the second entirely of our own making.

⌇⌇⌇⌇⌇⌇⌇⌇⌇⌇⌇⌇⌇⌇⌇⌇⌇⌇

Don't be afraid to make a mistake. The only thing we have to fear is our failure to correct it. Amelia Earhart writes, "The most difficult thing is the decision to act; the rest is merely tenacity."

⌇⌇⌇⌇⌇⌇⌇⌇⌇⌇⌇⌇⌇⌇⌇⌇⌇⌇

Early in life we make a mental list of the things we want. If we're fortunate, we won't get them until we can handle them.

Most of life's regrets come from the failure to begin the great idea of our lives. "Life is a direction," Carl Rogers teaches, "not a destination." It doesn't matter if we ever get there or not. What matters is that in trying to become one thing we wind up becoming exactly what we were most meant to be.

We are not just changing beings, we are learning beings. Every act of life is part of the process that makes us more and more our best selves. To ignore our responsibility to appraise each, and act accordingly in the future, is our greatest failure.

Education is not about a curriculum. It is about learning to learn. After that we can do anything, survive anything, become anything.

Life is a life-giving struggle. It is the gift that keeps us becoming more of the best we can be. It hones us to a new point and makes us standard bearers of the goodness of life.

Everything ripens at its time
and becomes fruit at its hour.

DIVYAVADANA

Spend a few minutes with this quote and then ask
yourself:

- What do these words say to me? What feelings or
  memories do the words evoke in me?

- What do these words say about my spiritual journey?

- My journal response to this quote is:

_____

The **Divyavadana** or **Divine Stories** or **Heavenly Deeds** is a Sanskrit collection of thirty-eight Buddhist stories from India that traveled throughout Asia, dating from as early as the second century. They are perhaps the first Buddhist texts to appear in written form.

Also by JOAN CHITTISTER

SONGS OF THE HEART
Reflections on the Psalms
HARDCOVER | 136 PAGES
$12.95 | 4" X 6" | 9781585958351

GOD'S TENDER MERCY
Reflections on Forgiveness
HARDCOVER | 80 PAGES
$10.95 | 4" X 6" | 9781585957996

THE SACRED IN-BETWEEN
Spiritual Wisdom for Life's Every Moment
HARDCOVER | 112 PAGES
$12.95 | 4" X 6" | 9781627850018

OUR HOLY YEARNINGS
Life Lessons for Becoming Our Truest Selves
HARDCOVER | 112 PAGES
$12.95 | 4" X 6" | 9781627850469

THE BREATH OF THE SOUL
Reflections on Prayer
HARDCOVER | 144 PAGES
$12.95 | 4" X 6" | 9781585957477

ASPECTS OF THE HEART
The Many Paths to a Good Life
HARDCOVER | 112 PAGES
$12.95 | 4" X 6" | 9781585958719